The Legend of Jimmy Drake

Written by Caitlin Fraser

Illustrated by Walter Carzon

Flying Start
to Literacy®

T0363489

Contents

Preface

This is a story about the brave men who built a railroad about 150 years ago, and the dangers and difficulties they had to overcome.

The railroad track was built from one side of the USA to the other. It was built over high, snowy mountains and across hot, dry deserts. It took more than six years to build, and hundreds of men died.

The men who built this railroad had to work hard in dangerous conditions, and only brave, strong workers could do it.

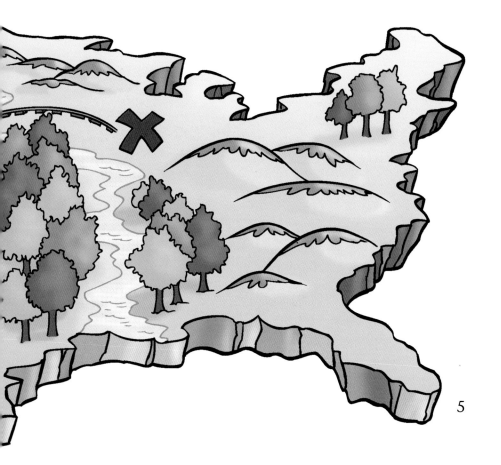

Chapter 1:

Avalanche!

Jimmy Drake and Lucas were working high in the mountains. They were surrounded by deep snow and it was bitterly cold.

"The bosses must be mad to think we can dig a tunnel through this mountain," said Lucas.

"At least we've got work so we can feed our families," said Jimmy Drake, and he began to whistle as he worked.

Then, without warning, a deep rumbling sound filled the air as snow, rocks and ice came roaring down the mountain.

"Avalanche!" yelled Lucas.

7

"Get out! Get out!" yelled Jimmy to the men inside the tunnel.

Jimmy and Lucas ran behind the railway cart, safe from the snow and rocks that were tumbling down the mountain.

The men inside the tunnel were not so
lucky. After the avalanche, the tunnel
was blocked by snow and huge rocks.

Five men were missing . . .
Five men were trapped in the tunnel!

Chapter 2:

Dig! Dig! Dig!

"Dig!" yelled Jimmy. "We have to get them out. Dig!"

Men came running from all over the camp. The men dug and dug. They were desperate to clear the snow and rocks that blocked the tunnel. They were desperate to save the workers trapped in the tunnel.

Hours went by, but the workers didn't stop.

"It's getting dark," said Lucas. "We have to hurry."

Finally, they saw a crack in-between two rocks.

"I can see inside the tunnel," said Jimmy.

"Hello!" the men yelled through the crack. "Hello! Hello! Can you hear us?"

Would the trapped men yell back? They waited, but there was only silence.

"They must have been killed," said Lucas.

"You don't know that," said Jimmy.

"Sorry Jimmy," said Lucas. "But there's
no hope."

One by one, the workers shook their heads
sadly, turned away and headed back
to camp.

"I'm not giving up," said Jimmy. "I'm going to move those rocks and get inside the tunnel."

"No," said Lucas. "It's not safe! You might get trapped too."

Inside the tunnel, the five trapped men were starting to lose hope. They were hungry and cold. And they were cut and bruised.

"They'll never find us," said one of the men. "We're in too deep."

As the hours passed, the men drifted in and out of sleep. They huddled together to keep warm.

Would anyone find them?
Would they be rescued in time?
Was anyone even looking for them?

Chapter 3:
Jimmy battles on

Outside the tunnel, Jimmy kept working into the night. Slowly and carefully, he moved rocks from the tunnel opening.   Finally, the small crack was big enough for him to squeeze through.

"One more rock to move," said Jimmy. "Then I'll be able to climb into the tunnel."

But, when Jimmy moved the last rock, more rocks came tumbling down around him. Once again, the tunnel was blocked.

"Oh, no!" sighed Jimmy.

Jimmy started to dig again.

By early morning, Jimmy had made a hole big enough to climb through.   Carefully, he made his way into the dark, dusty tunnel.

"Hello!" he yelled as he crawled along.

Soon, Jimmy came across another wall of rocks, a wall that stopped him from going any further.

There was no hope for the five men.

Chapter 4:
Safe at last!

Jimmy was about to give up when he heard a distant sound.

Tap! Tap! Tap!

It was coming from behind the rocks.

Jimmy tapped on the rocks with his pick.
He listened, and again he could hear
Tap! Tap! Tap! from behind the rocks.

Jimmy bolted from the tunnel and ran all the way back to camp.

"They're alive! They're alive!" he yelled.

Jimmy and the workers raced back to the tunnel.

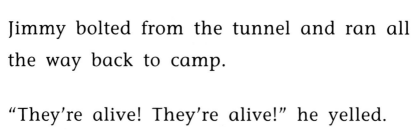

They kept digging until they finally reached
the five trapped men . . . alive and well.
And the story of brave Jimmy Drake has
been told ever since.

A note from the author

I once saw a documentary about the building of the transcontinental railroad in the 1860s. The railroad was built across the USA, and it took more than six years to build.

As I watched the documentary, I was staggered to hear that hundreds of men died while working on the railroad. These men must have been very brave to work in such harsh conditions.

The character Jimmy Drake came to life when I began to imagine what these workers might have gone through when there was an emergency such as a tunnel cave in. I hope you enjoyed the story!